# A Simpler Time

*by*
*Judy Condon*

## About the Author

Judy Condon is a native New Englander, which is evident in her decorating style and the type of antiques she collects and sells. Her real passion is for 19thC authentic dry red or blue painted pieces. While Judy's professional career was as an educator, Principal and Superintendent of Schools in Connecticut, her weekends were spent at her antique shop, Marsh Homestead Country Antiques, located in Litchfield, Connecticut.

When Judy's husband was relocated to Virginia, Judy accepted an early retirement from education and concentrated her energy and passion for antiques into a fulltime business. Judy maintains a website, http//www.marshhomesteadantiques.com and has been a Power Seller on eBay for over nine years under the name "superct".

With the success of her books and her working relationships with country shops throughout the United States and Canada, Judy has created a successful wholesale business of hand-poured primitive wax pieces and other handmade items that she sells wholesale to shops.

Judy has five children and five grandchildren. She lives in Spotsylvania, Virginia with her husband Jeff.

Judy's first two books *Country on a Shoestring* and *Of Hearth and Home – Simply Country* have been instant hits and are in their second printing. Judy may be reached through her website or her email address, marshhomestead@comcast.net

Library of Congress Cataloging-in-Publication Data
A Simpler Time/by Judy Condon
ISBN 978-0-9772309-3-8

Oceanic Graphic Printing, Inc.
105 Main Street
Hackensack, NJ 07601

Printed in China

Created, designed and typeset by Lisa Greenleaf, *Greenleaf Design Studio*
www.Lisagreenleaf.com

# Contents

## Dedication

My books could not have been created without the help of everyone who has allowed me into their home, been eager to share their ideas and encouraged me to "keep 'em coming". Thank you to my friend Gerri who travels with me down every road, even the dirt ones; Jan who lends an ear while volunteering her time; Connie who keeps me motivated with fresh ideas and feeds my soul; and Lisa, my designer, who sparkles with creativity. Special thanks to the love of my life, my husband Jeff, who is my unwavering source of encouragement, love and support. He allows me the time and space to fly at will but is there ready to pick me up if I fall.

# Introduction

Five years ago, I retired as a Superintendent of Schools in Connecticut when my husband was transferred to Virginia. I saw that as the opportunity to put into reality a book that I had been carrying around with me in my head for twenty years.

When I was first married and we were struggling financially to raise a family and "make ends meet", buying a box of Kleenex was a luxury. I, as many of us do when we first start out on our own, wanted a home that reflected my love of history, tradition and warmth.

Unable to do the things I wanted to do, I created ways to accomplish that goal in the least costly manner. Thus, my first book, **Country on a Shoestring**, became the collection of those ideas for decorating which impacted the overall affect of my home at a fraction of a cost. It was so well received with comments such as "finally something for the heart and soul of us who love country", that I created a second book, **Of Hearth and Home – Simply Country**. My second book contains photographs of 18th and 19thC homes from Nova Scotia to Arkansas and sold so quickly that it was reprinted within two months.

My emails and phone calls are all asking for more! Old friends, new friends and I'm sure the friends that I have yet to meet are calling to welcome me into their homes so that they can share and in turn benefit from others who are sharing. We are all thirsty for pictures that broaden our perspectives and provide new ideas through how others have decorated their homes at a time when little printed material is available.

I am one who loves to "wallow" in the beauty of pictures. As someone remarked to me "we lovers of country are a tribe and much larger than we imagine. Your books are giving us the chance to discover each other."

**A Simpler Time** is the third book in the series with a fourth book, **Country Decorating for All Seasons**, already planned and being written. A reader wrote to say, "It was raining here yesterday. I lighted all my candles, made a cup of tea, opened your book and was transported into country heaven".

So go put the kettle on, light those candles and take some time to escape for a few quiet moments to a simpler time.

# Chapter 1
# Log Homes

*"Come Along, come along, don't be alarmed.*
*United States is rich enough to give us all a farm"!*

*N*o period in American history has been more romanticized than that of life on the frontier. The romantic side of us would like to imagine early settlers living in a pristine log cabin on a peaceful grassy plain or at the foot of a tall mountain with billowing clouds overhead. In our mind, the cabin is filled with primitive furnishings, simple dripping candles and handmade quilts. Rather, the reality of the early log home is one of a dark building with gaping holes, falling pieces of dried dirt or clay, and overly crowded conditions.

*Ralph and Linda Miller's log home in Carroll Ohio*

*The log home of Dave and Twila Fairbanks near Roca Nebraska*

The Swedish and Germans are attributed with introducing the log home in North America in the late 1700s dispelling the theory that Pilgrims lived in log homes when they first arrived in the New World. The first log cabin typically consisted of one room that served as the kitchen, dining room and bedroom. It was a popular form of construction on the early frontier because homesteaders were able to readily find materials and a log home could be built in a matter of days with just the use of an axe and auger.

5

*Paul and Connie Pudelka's twenty two year old log home in Danbury Connecticut was built by Paul and his sons.*

Cost, rather than comfort, was the primary concern of the homesteaders and log cabins were cheap to build. Also, a log cabin could be abandoned if necessary without remorse.

The foundation was built with rocks and stone to keep the logs off the ground and prevent rotting. A crude rake was used on the dirt floor to keep it even and the roof was often sod. Chinking, a process of filling the spaces between the stacked logs with twigs, sod and chips of wood mixed with an adhesive compound of water and clay, helped to make the construction of the log home more durable. However, this process often resulted in providing ideal conditions for nests of bugs, insects and other "vermin".

The Homestead Act of 1862 greatly impacted the building of log homes. The United States government passed this act to promote expansion and offered any United States citizen 160 acres on which to build a home, improve the land and plant crops within a five year period. Everywhere reportedly, the song which was sung in

*Kyle and Nadine Brown's log home in Lebanon, Ohio. It sits on two acres of wooded property at the end of a long lane. Built of North Carolina square logs by Traditional Log Homes, it is fifteen years old.*

camps on the frontier was "come along, come along, don't be alarmed. United States is rich enough to give us all a farm". The Homestead Act specified some requirements for log cabins and mandated that they be at least ten by twelve feet in size and have at least one glass window. Although only approximately 30% of the settlers were successful in claiming their land permanently after five years, the log home remained the frontier home of choice until the late 1800's when, with the expansion of the railroad, materials such as timber and shingles became more readily available thus making it feasible to construct homes of board and batten.

The log homes in this book are a far cry from those mentioned above. All of the featured homes are large with many windows and all modern conveniences. Some of the log homes are occupied while others are used as outbuildings or shops. In some cases, the log homes were dismantled and moved, others were built from authentic early logs and some are newly constructed. The six log homes I'm including are those of Ralph and Linda Miller, Dave and Twila Fairbanks, Paul and Connie Pedulka, Kyle and Nadine Brown, Ron and Susan Derrow and David and Nancy Bryer.

*The side entrance to Ralph and Linda Miller's log home shown above is approached through a lovely flower and herb garden. The settee in blue paint on the porch is a new piece.*

*The "buttery" is the first thing you see upon entering from the side door. The standing dough box in dry apple green paint was found at the Springfield Antique Show. The buttery found in Nashville was purchased in its entirety and fits the space perfectly. Linda and Ralph have filled it with items indicative of the period; pantry boxes, crocks, firkins, and onion bottles.*

To the right of the entrance is the Miller kitchen, which was the first kitchen designed and built by Sally Whims. The superb "made to look old" dry blue paint is newly applied. Early cutting boards with rich patina hide the modern convenience of a sink. The hanging red cupboard may be a Sally Whims repaint but the apothecary on the counter in dry mustard paint is 19thC.

The large red cupboard built on site by the Whims, conceals the refrigerator. Next to it, a unique shaped 19thC cupboard in original paint most likely was from under a stairway judging by the angle of the top.

A rough-hewn barn board makes a perfect mantel. It holds a collection of vintage pewter and candlesticks. Early kitchen utensils, tin and treen, hang on pegs. Linda uses the oval pan, perhaps used in the 19thC by the Amish, to cook meat and vegetables. The fireboard was made by a neighbor and is used to keep the cold air out when the fireplace is not in use.

A two- board sawbuck table from New England holds an early bowl filled with primitive folk art fruit. The low settle is 19thC and also from New England.

*Sally Whims, restored the early 19thC pie safe with original tins in the Miller's Kichen.*

*The wrap around make-do chair was made by Judi Stellmach and Marion Atten of Blue Dog Antiques. Linda's favorite cupboard, in original paint, pictured right, houses her library.*

Jill Peterson hooked the folk art rug. The two-board early table retains original paint on the base and tapered legs. It was found in New England.

Vintage textiles in mustards and browns hang from an early drying rack in the hall. Below right, a miniature six-board chest from David Good with half moon ends and original leather straps sits atop an early jelly cupboard. The wooden ratcheted candlestick was a gift from Ralph's parents. The small oval pantry box is a new folk art piece. The portrait is unsigned but clearly 19thC.

Ralph and Linda use a 19thC rope bed in the master bedroom. Over the headboard, a hunt board holds a variety of vintage textiles.

A 19thC chimney cupboard holds Linda's collection of early textiles and quilts.

Off the master bedroom in a connecting alcove, the space is ideal for the early rope bed. The drop leaf table at the end of the bed, perhaps a salesman's sample or child's toy, was a gift from Ralph and Linda's son. The hanging corner wall shelf is a newly made piece done by Carolyn Thompson.

*Linda used a collection of vintage blue and white quilts in her guestrooms. Linen hung on hemp provides simple window treatments.*

Linens, textiles and a collection of albums are held on the shelves of the early cupboard in dry robins egg blue paint. Sitting atop the cupboard is Sir Arthur, a special bear to Ralph and Linda. While at a show, they approached a dealer to inquire if any of his bears was available for purchase. The dealer replied that he occasionally sells them but only to those he feels will take good care of them. The next day, Ralph and Linda were approached by the dealer and have felt honored that they were "approved and trusted" as the new owner of Sir Arthur.

The spinning wheel below is most likely a Canadian piece judging by the paint. Raw flax hangs from hooks and in the basket on the primitive bench.

The ogee mirror above is mid 19thC as is the original painted mustard dry sink which houses the sink in the Miller's first floor bathroom.

Linda and Ralph's shop *The Miller House* is a newly Amish built barn, which the previous owners lived in while the main house was being constructed. It is next to the main house, which adds convenience to Linda's availability for customers.

A smaller log cabin outbuilding was a gift Ralph and Linda gave to each other on their 35th anniversary. It was moved and reconstructed on the property and is an expansion of the shop.

Dave and Twila Fairbanks built their log cabin in 2002 shortly after 9/11 when they decided they wanted to move back to the prairie and be closer to family.

A 19thC corner cupboard sits behind an early table made of oak, walnut and pine. Early furniture makers used whatever wood they could find so it was not uncommon to find pieces constructed of a variety of woods. The table is pegged. The chairs are reproduction chairs made by Lawrence Crouse of Pennsylvania. On the table sits an early sifter holding a wreath, glass chimney and candle.

A Pennsylvania 19thC dry sink
with scalloped gallery and base,
sits behind a "floating" sofa in the
Fairbanks's living room. The early
jug on the floor is one of many items
Twila collects that have a star on it.

A red ware plate by
Greg Schooner sits
on top of a 19thC
Mennonite dry sink
in traditional mustard
over red dry paint.

Twila found the 19thC
apothecary with dry
attic surface in the
midwest.

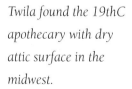

The four-drawer paint decorated chest to the right is a new piece made by Lawrence Crouse. The portrait, found in Pennsylvania above the chest, is the one piece Twila insists she would take if she could only take one piece in the room. Pictured to the right, an early pine worktable is set for intimate dining with treen plates and newly woven linen.

Starbucks in Kansas City made the pencil post bed in the Fairbank's master bedroom. The hooked rug over the bed was patterned after an early piece and is sold in Twila's shop Log Cabin Primitives and Woolworks. The coverlet, found in York County Pennsylvania, is dated 1846. The iron standing candlestick at the foot of the bed is a newly made piece by blacksmith artisan Kathy Nugent of Kansas. The pillows are covered with an early-initialed Lindsey-Woolsey blanket. The wreath against the pillow adds a homey touch at holiday time.

19

Vintage Amish knit stockings and capes hang from an old wardrobe peg rack create a striking silhouette against the logs and chinking in the master bedroom.

Woven linen secured with black carpenter tacks give the valence an older look in the Fairbanks' dining area. The windows overlook the arbor and herb gardens. The farm table is a new piece. The early trencher on the sideboard holds gourds from the garden.

The early painted chest in Paul and Connie's living room was found in Pennsylvania. The dry sink shown on the right was made by Paul, as was the table next to the wing chair. The early cradle dates to the 19thC and was found in Pennsylvania.

The window in Connie's kitchen provides a great deal of light despite the fact that almost the entire kitchen is wood. The counter tops are pine boards purchased at a local lumber store. Paul used a "biscuit" method to abut the boards. Drilling holes in the sides of the boards, he pegged them together then rounded the edges on the front. A Minwax® stain was applied once the boards were in place. Connie occasionally applies mineral oil, which is food safe, to protect the wood and maintain the patina.

The shelves on the back brick wall above enable Connie to display some of her extensive apple butter crock collection in graduated sizes. More butter crocks, red ware and Toby jugs are displayed on a reproduction red painted Stepback.

*Connie's sink below looks like it is a stone sink but it is a composition
material that she purchased at Home Depot®.*

*The basket below in Connie's keeping room adds texture to the pine walls. Hanging on the side of the brick fireplace is an early hay rake from which Connie has displayed assorted textiles.*

The bed in the Pudelka's guestroom is an early rope bed. The pull toy and bear are new pieces. The six board red chest was found in Pennsylvania. Below is a small sample of the large stoneware crock collection Connie has been gathering for over thirty years.

The master bedroom is carpeted for comfort but hopefully not for long according to Connie who is working on convincing Paul to replace the carpet with a wide plank floor. Connie was able to convince Paul to build a log home initially because of the low maintenance involved. The pine board walls and carpet certainly support this. The six-board chest at the foot of the bed has a smoke paint finish and was found in Pennsylvania. Connie made the small portrait to the left of the bed and was willing to share how it was done. The chapter Make A Portrait gives step-by-step instructions and pictures to help you make one for your home.

The dry sink on the right is a reproduction. The ladder-back chair in old paint was found in Connecticut. The table with remnants of white paint was found in Pennsylvania.

Empty nesters after thirty-five years, Connie converted their son's room into a guestroom. The maple bed is a new piece. Connie made the curtains from reproduction country blankets. Early textiles are displayed on a peg rack in the corner. To the left of the bed is an old wood box that Connie has inverted to create a bed table. Paul made the hutch table under the window.

*Nadine Brown bought the 19thC door for her home at a tag sale when someone said, "if you don't take it, I will"! Notice how the mirrored sconces are hung above the door to allow the door to open wide.*

*A six- board 18thC chest, most likely a grain bin, sits in the entrance of Kyle and Nadine Browns log home in Ohio.*

*The bin in dry red paint is constructed with rose head nails. Early dough boards and gourds surround a miniature six-board chest. An early mirror with original glass is hung over the end.*

*The dry red cupboard is early 19thC. An early treen bowl filled with soap sits on top. The mustard tin on the wall is the remnant of an early sconce.*

*The hanging cupboard above the stack of early chests is marked Portsmouth New Hampshire on the back. The lines of the arch half moon opening are what attracted Kyle and Nadine to the piece. Below the leather books, the middle shelf holds miniature pin cushions found in Pennsylvania and a reproduction watercolor print. A small dove tailed painted box sits on the bottom shelf.*

*More of Nadine's collection of leather books is nestled in a 19thC square nailed hanging shelf with an arched opening. The shelf is pine and retains its original red surface. Nadine finds leather books for $65 - $75. The color and patina determine which book Nadine decides to buy.*

An early dough board with rich patina hangs above the six-board blanket chest. Stone fruit, a 19thC hogscraper and stacked treen bowls complete the vignette.

The pewter cupboard on the right is early 1800's and is the original size as evidenced by the water stains at the base. The top shelf holds 17thC glass onion bottles, and an attic surface dome lidded box found in New England. The hornbeam on the side of the cupboard was used to store corn and to mash it in a similar fashion to that of a mortar and pestle. Above the cupboard, a make-do spoon rack made from a vintage cutting board with a board nailed across the front holds a collection of pewter spoons.

*Nadine has stacked a few of her early treen bowls on the top of a two- door 18thC pewter cupboard in red paint. The hanging apothecary above it with an early attic surface once held powder paints and is the one piece most customers try to buy when they come to the Brown home. It retains its original metal pulls.*

*Nadine found the 18thC open back buttery with dry red paint in New England. Collections of American treen plates, bowls, cupboard treen such as sugarers, mortars and pestles fill the shelves.*

*Reproduction bend
wood chairs surround
an early two-board
top sawbuck table.
A large early trencher
is filled with gourds
in the center. The
fireplace mantel
displays a row of
19thC hogscrapers.*

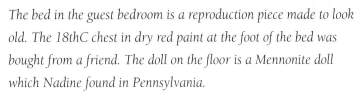

*The bed in the guest bedroom is a reproduction piece made to look
old. The 18thC chest in dry red paint at the foot of the bed was
bought from a friend. The doll on the floor is a Mennonite doll
which Nadine found in Pennsylvania.*

*The dry red two board top table with deep skirt is pegged. On the
top sits a few of the leather bound books Nadine collects. The one
to the far left is the oldest she owns. It is dated 1803 Massachusetts.*

The large bed in the master bedroom is a reproduction piece made by an artisan from Ohio. Above it hangs a unique signed wooden bed mat from the early 1800's. Originally the mat was placed on the ropes of the bed and beneath the straw mattress. The 19thC six board blanket chest in early red at the foot holds a treen bowl filled with sheep wool.

*The early red chest above holds, in addition to 19thC pantry boxes and a hogscraper, a bird made by Ginny Henson, a folk artist from Illinois who creates birds and animals.*

The log home of Ronnie and Susan Derrow in Mt. Sidney Virginia in the Shenandoah Valley was built in 1760. Susan is not afraid to mix periods and the final effect is stunning.

The clock, also made by Ronnie, is patterned after pieces made by Johannes Spitler who worked in Shenandoah County Virginia in the early 1800's. The large double stepback dates to the late 1800's and retains its original dry salmon paint. It was a built-in when Ronnie and Susan purchased it and without a back which Ronnie added.

The yellow pine pie safe in the dining room is circa 1850. It has turkey breast drawers and was found in Rockingham County Virginia. Susan uses the French cloche on top to protect her plants in the summer but moves it inside during the winter months. Ronnie made the bowl rack above which is filled with Lester Brenninger red ware from Pennsylvania.

The ten foot long walnut table in the Derrow's dining room is circa 1880. It was used for quilting in a Mennonite Church just outside Harrisonburg Virginia. After Ronnie and Susan got the table home, they discovered many pins still stuck in the cracks of it. The original stenciled chairs were made by the Spitler family of Maitland Virginia over generations. They are all similar in style but made of different woods.

Ronnie painted the front of the fireplace. Susan collects early copper pieces and has a large collection. The Federal mirror above the mantel is early 1800's.

Susan has collected early samplers for years and has at least twenty of them. She has a few in her collection that date to the 1700's. The early small dome box has a padded top and was most likely used for sewing. The miniature blanket chest is mid 1800's as is the mirrored sconce above it.

Susan leaves the early quilt hanging at the headboard year round, but changes the early quilt on the bed depending upon the seasons. The bed was a present to Susan on her sixteenth birthday from her parents. On either side of the bed is an early painted chest of drawers; one in black and one in red. The braided rug on the right side is turn of the century and was found in Kentucky. The outside is braided and the inside is a needlework pattern done with yarn. The cherry blanket chest with drawers holds a vinegar painted chest dating to the early 1800's.

Ronnie says the large 1820's armoire is staying with the house! It has been paint decorated with a comb but it is difficult to see the pattern. When purchased, one door was missing which Ronnie replaced. To this day, Susan says she can't remember which one was missing and can't tell.

Susan and Ronnie purchased the blue trundle bed from a traveling "picker" in Virginia about twenty years ago. When Ronnie's great Aunt came to visit, she thought the bed looked like one she had slept in as a child. Ron and Susan researched it and it turned out she was right! The tulip appliqué quilt is early. The early primitive doll's bed on the 19thC cobalt blue painted chest is where Nutmeg the cat sleeps.

An 1820's corner cupboard in dry blue paint holds a portion of Susan's quilt collection. The twig chair, an early one, is not only sturdy but also comfortable according to Susan.

The chest at the foot of the bed is an early box that Ronnie has painted in the style of Johannes Spitler. The square braided rug was "a must have" for Susan.

*The log home below was part of an old barn in Holland County Virginia. It is made of chestnut and was moved to the property in the early 1970's. Susan learned about the idea of stacking clay pots filled with succulents on an iron post at a garden club and couldn't wait to get home and add one to her herb garden.*

The log home below is used by Ronnie and Susan as an extension of their shop. Made of yellow pine, it dates to the 1700's and was moved to their property from New Hope Virginia. Because the original door was too small for most people to enter, they rotated the building, created a new door and used the original door as an entrance into the newly constructed addition.

An early yo-yo quilt square is used to dress up the window and still allow light to enter.

Ronnie uses old boxes that he paints in the Spitler style which they then sell in their shop, Shumake & Johnson.

Ronnie painted the fire screen right. The mantel, which Susan says they could have sold twenty times at least, is not for sale.

The small wall cabinet on the right in green and red is a copy of a Johannes Spitler piece that sold recently at Green Valley auctions in Mt. Crawford, Virginia for just under one million dollars.

Dave and Nancy Bryer moved last year from Connecticut to their Ohio log home that dates to the late 1800's. It is actually two log homes that have been moved and joined in between with an old buggy shed. Their master bedroom is up a few steps from one home and their children's bedrooms are up a few steps from the main floor of the adjoining cabin. On the side porch Nancy put the barrels in a corner when they moved in and "they've just stayed there". An early barn bench sits under an old tin lantern.

*Nancy has a passion for early apothecaries and you can find them throughout the cabins. This one in early white paint holds her collection of vintage books. Beneath it, the low red cupboard serves as a side table to the make-do chair. The table in front of the couch is an old New England bench.*

*Nancy has sold the make-do bench since this picture was taken. Her talented son makes many of the early primitive accessories and make-dos around the house. The ladder back chairs are new from The Seraph many years ago. The sawbuck table is early and was found in New England.*

Nancy's son dry scraped the cupboard right and discovered the dry blue under chrome yellow paint. Dave and Nancy found the old buttery counter in a barn in Connecticut where it was standing on end in a corner. Sally Whims painted the floor of the log home about fifteen years ago.

Dave and Nancy attached an old feed trough with remnants of early paint on the wall and fill it with bowls, buckets and treen. On the early bench with attic surface beneath, Nancy displays more of her painted firkins. Dried tobacco leaves hang on a hook above.

The make do desk is a two board table with original salmon paint. Found in New England, it has shoe feet and T nails.

A make-do wall table is in the keeping room. Nancy's son made the hanging wall shelf out of wide old boards. The hanging apothecary in mustard over red is a New England piece. Her son also makes reproduction treen plates similar to those on the wall shelf.

Nancy's kitchen was made by her son. He built the bottom cabinets which Nancy draped with linen indicative of the early log home kitchens where cupboard doors didn't exist and fabric was used to keep the critters away. The hanging blue cupboard looks to be a fragment of a larger piece.

The room shown on the left will be converted into a full-scale buttery in the next few months. The robins egg blue bench is from Massachusetts. In the back corner, an early apothecary with missing drawers has been made into a wine rack storing bottles of wine in the spaces where the drawers are no longer there.

## Chapter 2

# Bedrooms

*"Always Kiss Me Goodnight"*

*F*or years my husband and I struggled with an early double sized bed because I was too stubborn to consider a larger size that didn't fit our "early decor." Now, many companies and craftsmen are making beds that are perfect replicas in a variety of styles. Some of the pictures of bedrooms have old beds while others are reproductions. It's hard to tell the difference! In either case, often quilts, early textiles and accessories help to blend the new with the old.

Jean Peterson refers to the room on the previous page as the children's room. The early "hired hand" bed is covered in a 19thC coverlet. A hired hand bed was a "stripped down" version of a normal bed. It had posts and rails but no headboard or footboard. Red and white quilts give the room a patriotic theme. Shown on the right, vintage toys fill the cupboard shelves. Jean has spelled the names of her children and grandchildren using old printers blocks. A handcrafted folk art Noah's Ark sits a top a miniature 19thC six-board chest at the foot of the bed.

*Jean displays vintage clothing on the closet doors of the room. The small dress in the middle was her dress as a child. On the shelf over the three-drawer pine chest is a collection of Raggedy Ann and Andy dolls from the 1930's.*

The early pineapple post twin beds in the Ramsey's guestroom work beautifully together although they were found separately. The coverlets are new. The throws at the foot of each bed are old Army blankets. The chest in between the beds is 19thC with an original dry red wash surface.

Anita and Gerry Ramsey were given the pineapple post bed on the right from a friend. The textile coverlet is a new piece woven by Family Heirloom Weavers of Pennsylvania.

*The Ramsey's guestroom was formerly the master bedroom before they added a master bedroom on the first floor. The armoire is an early oak piece that was a family heirloom. The small sawbuck table is newly made from old wood with original early dry mustard paint. The chest under the window holds linens and was an early tool chest.*

Arnette loves early blue paint! Here in each of the Droit's guestrooms, early blue pieces hold rocking horses. The mule chest in original blue was found in Ohio. Early German mohair bears are seated on the folky early rocking horse.

*Above an early rope bed in red wash is covered with a 19thC patchwork quilt. Underneath the bed is an early trundle bed with wooden wheels. The blue pie safe was found in Indiana. The chairs above the bed are early dollhouse chairs. The gameboards are reproductions.*

*Sharon DiCampo purchased her pencil post bed from The Keeping Room in Douglas Massachusetts. The plaid wool blanket was purchased in Sturbridge. The shelf over the bed holds leather books and a small feather tree in a miniature doll's cradle.*

*The red wash hanging cupboard above was made from old wood and displays some of Sharon's German stick-legged sheep collection. Sharon has had the small bear since childhood. The large 19thC cupboard on the left hides a wide screen television and DVD player.*

Below a two door early red paint cupboard holds an open shelf with vintage linens and textiles.

*Louise and Ralph Villa's bedroom has a working fireplace. The pencil post bed is a reproduction purchased at The Keeping Room in Douglas MA. Early woolen blankets sit on the chest at the foot of the bed. The room is large enough to accommodate a large spinning wheel in the corner.*

*One of two guest rooms at the Villas is shown on the left. Warm blankets and a candle in the window welcomed us on a snowy wintry night*

The Peterson's cat Brecka was not the least bit phased by the intrusion. The 19thC cherry bed is a new acquisition and will be dressed with a canopy. Jean's research on her 1740's home shows that the first two owners, Dr. William Jennison and Rev. Isaac Stone were wealthy and influential in town. Jean has decorated this guestroom in a period indicative of how it would have looked in the mid 18thC.

At the opposite corner of the room, Jean displays early textiles, samplers, and a hooked rug. Next to the spinning wheel is an 18thC candle stand and a full-sized adult "potty" chair for those early nights when a trip outside was to be avoided. The Peterson house was part of the Underground Railroad and during restoration. Jean and Paul found an area next to the fireplace in this room where slaves would have been hidden. It is behind the door to the chimney cupboard. The parson's cupboard over the mantel holds a collection of books.

*John and Barbara's shop, Good Old Days, carries both antique and reproduction pieces. Above, the bed is from Shaka Studios, the furniture from Pocono Primitives, the ottoman from Johnston Benchworks and the fabrics from Family Heirloom Weavers. The Good Old Days website is www.goodolddayscountryshop.com.*

Pam Parker has covered her reproduction bed with an early quilt and a coverlet purchased at The Keeping Room in Douglas. The canopy is made of wool sheets which Pam cut in half and then draped over the frame. The recessed wall cupboard houses their television. The small vase with berries adds a nice touch between the two windows.

## Chapter 3
# Kitchens
### "Kissin' don't last. Cookin' do"
—From the Amish

*I*'ve received a number of requests to include in my next book a chapter on kitchens. It seems we're all looking for ways to decorate the room in the house where we spend so much of our time.

*Carolyn Thompson loves primitives and it is especially evident in her kitchen. Her stone sink is ideal for the overall effect. The dry New England cupboard with rose head nails in old red hangs above early mortars and pestles, some still retaining original bark,*

Carolyn purchased the Massachusetts apothecary for the original putty color paint which matches the stone sink in color. An old leather and wooden butcher's carry case, which Carolyn uses to hold knifes, hangs next to the apothecary.

*Sally Whims created the primitive kitchen above and designs custom kitchens which are sold through Old Glory in Waynesville Ohio. Bea Sparrow, owner of Old Glory, uses the area to display vintage baskets, treen and pantry boxes. Although newly created pieces, each certainly has the primitive early look we seek in our homes and demonstrates how we can blend authentic and replica pieces if necessary.*

*Carolyn's period hanging candle holder has its original iron hook. The buttery shelves are early and New England.*

*Another of Donnie and Sally Whims kitchen design is shown on the right. Most of us would be hard pressed to question the authentic surface of the hanging cupboard.*

*Stacee Droit gravitates towards original blue paint. Here, the 19thC blue dry sink was found in Indiana. Above it hangs an early Amish cheese cupboard from Kentucky. A graduated set of fly screens sits in between. The pine apothecary in the background has a natural patina. The milk cupboard beneath kept flies off the milk as it cooled.*

The large cabinet in Stacee's kitchen is a TV cabinet which Stacee's husband Bruce adapted to hide a microwave and dishwasher. Stacee uses the early standing dough box in dry blue paint as an island. A grain painted wall cupboard to the left of the sink holds spices.

The table in Bruce and Stacee's kitchen is an early hutch table in green paint. Bruce made the window treatments with ripped boards that he hinged together.

*A small cupboard on Jim Hohnwald and Bob Jessen's kitchen counter holds a late 18thC George Washington commemorative red ware plate. The basket on top is a mid 19thC double handled Indian basket in original paint with potato stamping. The carrier on the middle shelf in blue and white is from Maine. The small coffin shaped stool was found in New Hampshire.*

*Jean and Paul Peterson have a winter and summer kitchen. Pictured above, the summer kitchen was originally part of the milkhouse. The cupboards and, in fact all of the Peterson's woodwork, have been refinished with a process of using a walnut stain and latex paint. After stripping the wood, Jean and Paul applied a coat of special walnut stain which they then wiped off. A coat of flat latex paint was applied. When dry, a small sander was used to distress "wear" on the wood. A final coat of stain was then applied and rubbed down. The hooked rug above the antique cast iron sink is a late 19thC piece.*

Jean and Paul are the sixth owners of their home. The small window in the summer kitchen is one of the original windows to the house. The small box hanging on the wall is early. The three drawer small chest is a reproduction. Some of Jean's red ware collection is displayed on the shelves.

*Jean used the same process in finishing the cupboards in her winter kitchen which was formally the birthing room. This kitchen houses the "kitchen conveniences" such as stove and dishwasher, keeping them concealed from the rest of the house. In the cupboards above, Jean displays some of her extensive yellowware collection. She particularly likes blue-banded yellowware.*

The hanging shelf in blue is a reproduction. A display of tombstone, round and unique pointed dough boards surround it. The large round cutting board resting in the center on the counter is German.

Hidden behind the cupboard door is the refrigerator. The alcove above is a perfect display space for salt glazed stoneware. The small shelf in blue paint contains a set of matched blue- banded yellowware custard cups. In the small box below it, Jean displays a miniature child's masher and rolling pin.

## Chapter 4

# Comfortable Settings

*"I sat some minutes lost in my thoughts of the beauty of the place".*
—William Orville Douglas

*O*ftentimes I am not sure of how a book will evolve until I have taken my photographs and gone through them many times to fine tune them and make the final decision as to which will be included or saved for a later time.

I realized that I had captured many photos of quiet settings where perhaps someone could just sit, write a letter or appreciate "the beauty of the place." In each case, the photo spoke of a simpler time when the pace was slower and a sense of calm prevailed. The beauty to my eye is in the simplicity of the "place" that has been captured on film.

*The early 18thC ladder back in original paint is from coastal New England and still has its original rush seat. The X-base candle stand in old red paint is circa 1750 and most likely originated in coastal New Hampshire.*

*Shown in a corner of Jim and Bob's kitchen area is a Chippendale ribbon back armchair circa 1760.*

*The two- door 18thC hanging cupboard to the left retains its original snipe hinges. Nadine Brown found the ladder back chair in New England. Having four slats date it to the late 1800's. The make-do candle stand with Massachusetts provenance has been made with an old wood base and the top of an early hogscraper embedded into it.*

*Nadine Brown found the three drawer black chest at the Richmond Illinois show traditionally held the first Saturday in June. The chair is an 18thC ladder back with mushroom-capped arms. The chair was covered in quilted fabric by Judi Stellmach Of Blue Dog Antiques in Stafford Springs, Connecticut. She and her partner, Marion Atten of Illinois, make these chairs in either vintage Lindsey-Woolsey or quilted fabrics.*

*Carolyn Thompson's sofa is a 1700's piece found at the Heartland Show last fall in Richmond Indiana. Contrary to what you might think, it is not a make-do but rather an original frame that has been slip covered. It works nicely with the early pegged swing leg table found at Brimfield. Remnants of original salmon paint can be seen underneath when the leg swings out.*

A row of hogscrapers with douters create an artistic silhouette against the wall on the mantel. A fire in the fireplace invites everyone to sit and enjoy.

Adapted from an early wooden chair, the "wrap around" chair was used to further create a spot of warmth on cold days next to the fire. The fabric has been distressed to blend with the period chair. The hanging Betty oil lamp hangs from an X-base stand once used to hold a rush light. Carolyn found them together at Heart O Country.

The period Windsor chair on the right is intact and is part of a make-do. The entire chair was added to a base; perhaps to allow the owner to sit at a high desk. Note the worn rung in the front. The hanging flat-top tin lantern is early 1700's. A wig stand is visible on top of the bookcase that has been filled with early leather-bound books.

The early New England tree hook holds a powder horn, and an early sheep's wool bag from Carolyn Thompson's frontier collection. On the stand sits an early treen container with quills.

The board and batten door with dry attic surface leads nowhere but could not be passed up. Carolyn found the three-legged candle stand in Cape Cod and believes it had been used by a sailmaker as it still has remnants of black tar and sailmaker's chain.

The early weaver's bench from New Hampshire rests in Carolyn's kitchen. Note how worn it is on one side from use.

*Carolyn has created an authentic frontier look in her home in Ohio. The iron utensils are ones she has used to cook with when preparing a fireplace meal. The ladder back above with vertical slats is a reproduction chair patterned after an 18thC chair with New England origin.*

*Carolyn bought this wonderful period settee, sold it and bought it back! Above it hangs an early tin sconce from New England and an old musket. The X-base stand is actually a cobbler's stand that Carolyn has filled with old music and an early flute. The leather frontier bag is made of a lighter color hide and blends with the color and patina of the powder horn.*

The desk above in the Droits study is a
two-board table, which has been made
into a desk with a make-do gallery. The
black bucket bench from Pennsylvania
holds a mustard piggin from New England
and early beeskep. The hanging rack is
actually an old grain bowl rack filled
with treen and small pantry boxes.

From New England, the 19thC
hanging desk has original cobalt
blue paint. The chair next to it is
a spinning chair, which is taller
than the average chair. Just barely
visible is an old gameboard in
dry paint.

*Bruce and Stacee Droit call this room the tavern room. A primitive sawbuck table holds wick trimmers and a stone pear on a leather book. An early spinning wheel is tucked in beside the armchair draped with a Woolsey blanket.*

*An early fruit dryer is placed next to the fireplace where it would have been found in the 19thC.*

*Jim and Bob's hanging shelf on the right came out of a home in a neighboring town. It is circa 1840's and judging by the marks left on the wall, when it was removed, it had been in the same spot since it had been made. The small buildings on the top shelf are early cast iron banks. The gameboard below it in early paint is 19thC*

*Beneath the upholstery, the wing back chair is second period and has a dovetailed frame. The decoy on the table in early paint is a redhead and one of Bob's collections.*

Pictured on the left, Jim and Bob's
18thC Windsor armchair is typical
New England in its severe style. The
Windsor candle stand is a dish top style,
so named because of the rim around the
edge. The onion bottle is early 18thC
and is either Dutch or English. These
bottles originally held beer which were
delivered by the thousands of bottles to
the fort at British Guinea. After they
were emptied, the bottles were thrown
over the walls and into the river which
is where many have been found.

*The edge of an early 19thC child's chair is seen in the corner and creates a pleasant visual line against the early window. The fire bucket signed W Marsh is purported to be a Connecticut piece. The early rush light is 18thC and unique in that it also has a candle socket.*

*The make-do chair was made by Blue Dog Antiques and is in the keeping room of Nancy and David Bryer's 17thC log home.*

*The red wash gate leg table in the center of the sitting room of Jim and Sandy O'Connor's lake house is mid 19thC. The cheese strainer on the wall was found in CT. The cupboard with remnants of blue paint on the door is also from New England. Sitting on the top is an early tool carrier in dry blue paint found in Massachusetts. The mustard sign is actually an old sign which has been newly repainted. The hunt board in the corner holds early linen textiles. The old blue butter churn in front of the cupboard is one of two Sandy owns.*

*Rich Lortie made the highboy against the wall indicative of the Williamsburg style he prefers. He also created the floor cloth painted by his wife Melanie. And early onion glass bottle sits on the 1700's round table purchased in Massachusetts.*

Chapter 5

# How to Weave a Shaker Cloth Seat

*A*t flea markets and tag sales, I've found it is relatively easy to find ladder back chairs with cane or rush seats in need of repairs; sometimes for as little as $10. Although the Shakers were known for their conservative and dark colors of dress, they often used brighter colors in the weaving of their chair seats. I have woven my seats in burgundy and tan and in blue and tan at a cost of approximately $25-$30 per chair. H.H. Perkins Company, Inc. in Connecticut is an excellent source for the tape. They can be reached at 800-462-6660 or HPerkinsco@aol.com.

## You will need the following materials:

- Approximately 34 yards of 1" tape or 40 yards of 5/8" tape (17 or 20 yards of each color if you are going to do a checkerboard pattern)
- Scissors
- carpet tacks
- hammer
- dull edged dinner knife
- square piece of foam padding

## Step 1 _____

After you have removed the old seat and repaired any loose or broken wooden parts, you're ready to begin. Tack the end of the darker color tape of the two tapes, to the underside of the left rail next to the back left chair leg. You are starting to create what is called your warp strips.

## Step 2

Pull the tape under the back cross piece and towards the front of the chair. Loop the tape over and then under the front crosspiece and bring it to the back rail. Go under then over the back rail. Continue in this manner until you have wrapped the warp strips entirely across the front rail of your chair. You need to be certain that the strips are not overlapping, are tight and are in a straight line running horizontally at right angles between the front and back rails. When you have covered the front rail and have no room left for another warp on the back, tack the end of the warp to the underneath side of the right side rail at the back right post.

You will notice that you have two front corners without a warp, as the front of the seat is wider than the back.

## Step 3

Cut two pieces 3" longer than the distance between the front rail and the back post. Turn the chair over and tack one end of the strip on the underside of the front chair rail. Pull the tape back and tack it to the underside of the left chair rail at the back left leg. Do the same thing on the right side. This will fill in the corners across the front.

Your seat should look as it does in the picture below.

## Step 4

Insert your piece of foam padding between the top and bottom layers of your warp. This will soften the seat and tighten your warp at the same time.

From the side, it will look as it does in the picture on the right.

## Step 5

Now you're ready to begin your weave with the lighter color tape. This is called the weft tape. Turn your chair upside down so that the front of the seat is resting on your lap. Start at the back left corner on the underneath side of the seat. Leaving about 3" of your tape as a tail, start and go over the first warp strip, then under the next and alternate until you get to the other side of the chair.

## Step 6 ———————

Flip the chair over and continue on the topside of your seat making sure that you are going over the first and under the second all the way across the chair. After I have pulled the weft through each row, I push the row back across the previous row so that the rows are even. If you do this as you complete each row, it will be easier than waiting until you have finished.

As you get closer to the front of the seat, it becomes very tight and difficult to weave the weft strips over and under the warp. Using a dull edge dinner knife, I fold the strip so that there is a loop at the end of it and use the knife to push it over and under the warp.

## Step 7 _____

After you have woven the last row of weft, turn the chair over and weave the "tail" into the warp on the underside of the seat.

Turn the chair over and weave the tail of the other end of the weft in the warp at the back of the seat underneath. Your seat will last for years and when it gets soiled, pull off the tape, turn it over and weave the seat again with the clean side up.

## Chapter 6

# Dining Rooms

*"Give Us This Day. . ."*

*The period hutch table right from Massachusetts retains original salmon paint. It is constructed with rose head nails and has a scrub top*

*B*efore the days when Malls were open on Sunday and that day of the week became as any other, my family traveled a half hour to the home of my maternal grandparents each week. It was a tradition that represents some of my fondest memories as a child.

We would pile in the car; my brother, sister and I arguing over which one of us would have to sit in the little pull down seat in the back. It was a time when I recall my Dad playing Chinese checkers with us and my grandfather teaching me how to play Canasta while my less than five foot tall Grammy made homemade dumplings in the kitchen to serve with the roasting chicken.

Of course my grandfather sat at the head of the table while my seat was to his immediate left; something I have grown to treasure as a place of honor. Dinner became a quiet family time that even after decades

my five senses occasionally help me to recall. To this day, there are times when the experience of eating a particular food, smelling a particular aroma or hearing a bell similar to that which called us to the table will take me back to that simpler time.

Although none of the dining rooms resembled that of my grandparents', the tranquility of the settings in the following photographs remind me of days long ago.

*Jim and Bob's table is set with broad check linens. The sign over the mantel is an old tavern sign dating to 1840 in old red and black paint. It reads Monroe Hotel by John Goff. The stars on either side of the word "by" and the moons on either side of "John Goff" have been interpreted to mean "by day and night."*

A period table shown on the left is in Carolyn's "ship room". The entire room began with the oil on canvas painting that Carolyn could not pass up. The suspended folk art carved fish is an early trade sign from Maine in original seafoam blue green paint.

Bea Sparrow of Old Glory in Ohio mixes old and new pieces in her shop. The early drop leaf pine pegged table welcomes guests into a dining room setting. The fireboard is one of Sally Whims. The lantern above the mantel is early as is the standing Betty oil lamp on the table.

The Droits found the large sawbuck pegged and square nailed table in Kentucky. The cupboard in the background holds some of Stacee's large collection of early painted smalls. The Windsor chairs are new.

*Blue salt glazed stoneware are displayed in the tall 19thC cupboard with canted back and single board doors. In the Droit's dining room, the dough box on top has original blue paint. Although the hanging candle rack looks like a make-do, it is early.*

*The Droit's found the magnificent 19thC blue cupboard in Illinois an the dough box in cobalt blue in Kentucky. The canvas decoy is circa 1920's.*

*Sandy and Jim O'Connor created a corner cupboard by standing a large cattle trough on end. An early wooden bucket filled with some of Sandy's treenware, is on the third shelf. Sandy displays new and old baskets from the beams.*

*The O'Connor's lake house on Bantam Lake in Connecticut is finished in natural pine horizontal boards allowing the eye to focus on the furniture and textures while minimizing the upkeep. One of Sandy's favorite pieces is the early standing dough box in original red paint purchased in Connecticut.*

Jim and Bob's seven-foot long 18thC sawbuck table has a single board top and old red base. Pinned and constructed with rose head nails, the stretcher on the table is dovetailed into the legs. The table is indicative of the early American pieces in which Jim and Bob specialize. The chairs are an original set of New England side chairs and date to the late 18thC. The table is set with treenware plates, noggins and pitchers. A hanging lantern in dry olive paint with original glass is almost identical to one at Sturbridge Village in Massachusetts.

*Sunshine casts an interesting light on Al and Ann Kuehn's dining room corner. The dough bowls in early paint above the mantel are displayed in a bowl rack made by Ann's husband, Al. The picture on the following page shows the original red paint of the table.*

*Ann uses an early hutch table as a bench. The Windsor chairs are reproductions.*

*Jim and Ruth Rochelle's newly added Tavern Room used to be their dining room and is now their favorite room in the house. The wood for the room was purchased in Connecticut and came out of a 19thC house that was being torn down. Some boards still had rose head nails imbedded in them. The sawbuck table with original salmon paint was found in Pennsylvania and is pegged. The chairs are reproductions. Ruth painted the floor and stenciled it in a dark mustard and black.*

The Rochelle's found the early wall cupboard in Ohio but were told it originally came from the East. They later found out that it actually dates to circa 1790 and came out of a tavern in New England. The plate rack holds a collection of pewter tankards and measures.

*Early tin ware and freshly canned jars of preserves sit on Shannon McConnachie's two-board scrub top table*

*Judy Coffey's keeping room is the first room you step into upon entering the house. The early blue gray painted table was found in Connecticut. The ladder back chair is early as is the old green painted bench. On the table sits a Tommy Sticking candleholder used in the mines in the 19thC.*

*The apothecary on the left side of the mantel is 19thC and holds some of Judy's stoneware collection. In front of it, a tall firkin with natural patina was purchased as a make-do churn but Judy preferred to leave the top open.*

*Judy's taste has evolved into an appreciation of early paint and as you move through her home, there are many elements of a red, white and blue theme. Over the mantel, Judy has placed a flag. Her extensive pewter collection is lovely against the red background. The 19thC candle box in original paint has a heart cutout and is most likely a Pennsylvania piece.*

*The large Stepback in old red paint came right out of a house in Massachusetts. Judy was fortunate to also purchase the hanging red cupboard next to it from the same owner. In the tilted dough box on top, Judy displays a yellowware batter bowl and pitchers. A red scale is to the side on the top shelf. Judy has a large collection of firkins and mixes painted with original surface pieces in her collection.*

*Judy has mixed early pieces with dry red, white and blue paint in her keeping room. The sifter on top of the red hanging cupboard is Shaker..*

The dough bowl hanging on the top in the picture to the right, is a large early piece in old red paint with a wonderful repair. A stack of bail handled pantry boxes are on top of the large 19thC cupboard in early red.

The table and chairs in Judy's dining room are DR Dimes reproductions. A friend painted the canvas floor cloth. Judy has stacked benches in the back to create space for her early dough box which is filled with dough bowls.

The pine pie safe in the back of the picture is 18thC and still retains its original snipe hinges.

*One of Judy's favorite pieces is the half measure in early mustard paint filled with Belini apples.*
*Judy found the 19thC cabinet in original red with blue gray at Brimfield. A vintage hooked rug*
*of The Three Bears can be seen on the wall behind the early bench.*

Melanie and Rich Lortie had a tinsmith from Sturbridge Village make their lighting. The wall sconce is one example of the 19thC replica lighting pieces found throughout their home.

The Lortie's have combined their many talents to create a home that is clearly comprised of pieces made with their hands and hearts. Rich made each piece of furniture in the dining room while Melanie did the finishing work on the furniture, painted the floor cloth, and did the stenciling. The paint on the inside of the cupboard is an Old Village® paint called Antique Pewter.

# Chapter 7
# Folk Art

*"Art is the desire of a man to express himself, to record the reactions of his personality to the world he lives in"*

—Amy Lowell, poet 1874-1925

*Ronnie Derrow made the folk art figure for Susan's garden. It was created from a Dean Johnson pattern.*

*F*olk art provides us with the ability to trace our history and ancestry as it oftentimes is indicative of a particular culture or society. Folk art is quite different from formal art as it evolved out of a necessity in life and was created by ordinary "folk" who were without formal "institutionalized" instruction or training. A good example of folk art is that of the quilt which served a specific utilitarian function but was aesthetically beautiful. Oftentimes a quilt will have specific characteristics or patterns which educate us to something about the culture or society to which the quilter may have belonged.

Folk art is becoming more popular today than ever before and encompasses many forms and styles. Weathervanes, gameboards, quilts, birdhouses, and signs are but a few examples of folk art which continue to escalate in price and value for collectors. Folk art shows continue to draw large crowds seeking the unique piece. The tradition of folk art shows occurring in the fall continues as it had originated. When the planting and harvesting was completed for the season, the common folk could devote his time to the creation of that utilitarian piece which in years to come would become a highly valued piece of art.

*Susan and Ronnie's Noah's Ark collection is displayed in their living room. Folk artist Nancy Thomas of Yorktown Virginia made the ark on top. The others are German, made from cardboard and date to the 1920's*

*German stick-legged wooly sheep in various sizes have become popular collectors items as well as early children's toys such as the pull toy stick-legged sheep above.*

*A trio of early decoys in early paint sit on a unique three-tiered hanging shelf. Hand-carved decoys are highly sought after and can cost anywhere from $100 to thousands.*

Shannon McConnachie made the doll pictured on the left. Shannon was named by Early American Life as one of the top folk artists of the year. Her home also appeared in my second book *Of Hearth and Home – Simply Country*. Another example of her creative folk art is the log cabin.

Vintage hooked rugs are becoming increasingly popular and hard to find. The newly hooked rug pictured below was done by Jill Peterson.

An early set of carpet bowling pins are today classified as "folk art".

Quilts and hooked rugs such as those shown right and below are sold at Old Glory in Waynesville Ohio.

*Early wooden signs in old paint are favorites and sell quickly at Bill Quinn's shop in Alna Maine. Sometimes utilitarian pieces such as early wooden wheels are displayed in a special manner and become forms of folk art. The early water sprinkler in the center is a rare collector's item.*

Ann Kuehn discovered the "Buy Hackney Wagons sign" when she had just moved into her new home and was cleaning the floor. She looked up and discovered that the underside of three pantry shelves were old painted signs. Ann did some research and learned that there had been a general store located across the street at one time and they had sold Hackney Wagons. The fact that Outzville is misspelled on the sign may be the explanation as to why the signs ended up as shelves in the pantry.

Carved folk art birds sit on an early apple green table in Ralph and Linda Miller's bedroom.

*Ann Kuehn found the early rocking horse in New England and the sign behind it in Pennsylvania.*

*Bruce and Stacee Droit enjoy collecting vintage toys. They found the blue wagon seat in Pennsylvania. The shelf, found in Missouri, holds an old mohair elephant pull toy, tin horns and a print cat.*

*Drums and early bears, some dating to the 19thC, sit on the bittersweet wash 19thC cupboard.*

*A 19thC wagon seat in early red paint holds a vintage cloth doll.*
*The rocking horse is one of many Bruce and Stacee Droit collect.*

*Carving birds is a hobby of Bob Jessen in New Hampshire. These sit in a window adjacent to Jim and Bob's driveway adding a welcoming touch to visitors and customers.*

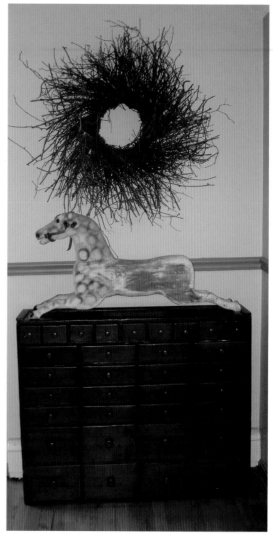

Many children's toys have become collectibles as folk art. These rocking horses owned by Judy Coffey are most likely German. The mustard store counter top was found at Brimfield and makes an ideal cupboard for displaying some of Judy's yellowware.

*Jim Hohnwald has been collecting vintage tin cookie cutters and chocolate molds for almost thirty years. The large heart is 19thC which Jim bought about 27 years ago. The 19thC Christmas tree has been in his collection for almost the same amount of time. The belsnickel chocolate molds are turn of the century.*

## Chapter 8
# Stencils and Murals

*I*n my first book, Country on a Shoestring, I talked about the impact stencils can have on the overall affect of a room. They add color, pull the various colors in a room together and can give the optical illusion of lowering a ceiling level to create a warmer more intimate feeling in the room.

In the picture below, stencils have been used to create a floor cloth appearance. It was not uncommon in the 19thC to paint the floor and stenciling today has become a popular form of creative expression. The secret to a successful floor stencil is the preparation and measuring. First and foremost is to be certain that your floor is clean. Using your stencil size as a guide, measure out your squares starting from the center of the desired area to be stenciled. This will help insure that the overall stencil is positioned in the center of your room.

Work from the inside out. You can make your stenciled area as large or as small as you choose. You can always add another surrounding row of stencils if you decide at some point that you want a larger area. When you have finished, and once

your paint is dry, apply three coats of polyurethane to protect and seal your floor.

Achieving the look of an early 19thC original wall is not a difficult task. The

following process will give a new wall the look of a 19thC aged wall. Using an ecru or light off-white color latex paint, prepare and paint your room. Select a stencil, which will provide you with a larger pattern such as the pineapple shown on the next page

Divide your wall in sections and vertically mark each section. Position your stencil in the center of the section. The key to a successful project is again taking the time to measure and mark your surface before you begin.

131

Using a stencil with a coordinating border is helpful for filling in smaller spaces such as over doorways and windows.

Using a damp sponge and antique glazing compound, randomly sponge your walls. You can also use a Ralph Lauren® stain called Tobacco Tea Stain available at Home Depot®. This will give your walls an aged look similar to that of a tea-dyed fabric or old plaster wall.

In the early 19thC, itinerant artists would travel from home to home and, for often times as little as $10, paint a mural on a wall. Rufus Porter is perhaps the most famous artist whose works have been uncovered on walls in Maine and New Hampshire during renovations of early properties. Guy Paulin of Maine has achieved the Rufus Porter look on the stairwell leading up to the second floor of Guy and Debbie's home. The mural depicts early scenes from the Portsmouth New Hampshire harbor and surrounding area. Guy's large mural over his fireplace is featured on the cover of my second book *Of Hearth and Home–Simply Country*. Guy paints the murals freehand using acrylic paint and then glazes the surface.

Susan Dwyer of The Painted
Colonial Studio painted the mural
in one room of Robin Rock's shop,
Milltown Primitives, located in
the historic seafaring town of
Old Mystic Connecticut.

Gladys Desmond of Rhode Island,
painted the mural to the right
for Kate Foynes, owner of The
Keeping Room, a large country
shop in Douglas Massachusetts.
Contact information for Itinerant
Painter. Ms Desmond's business,
can be found at the back

## Chapter 9
# Creating a Portrait

𝒰sing a print to create a reproduction oil on canvas is an inexpensive way to enjoy an early portrait until you can purchase an authentic 18ᵗʰ or 19ᵗʰ oil portrait. And it's easy to do!

## Step 1:

Purchase a print from an art shop or from the internet. Buy a stretched canvas on a frame from your local craft store that is identical in size to the picture portion of your print. You will need a brush, opaque black acrylic paint from a craft store, spray adhesive and either an antiquing stain, available through your local paint store, or Brie® wax.

## Step 2:

Cut the print to fit your canvas. Spray your adhesive on the canvas and glue your print to the canvas. Using a roller, press the print to the canvas. I placed weights on my print to further apply pressure.

## Step 3:

When dry, paint the edges of the canvas with the black paint and allow time to dry.

## Step 4:

Using Brie® wax or an antiquing glaze, rub the compound lightly over the print. This will give it a glossy appearance similar to an oil portrait.

*Connie Pedulka made these two "canvas portraits" which hang in her log home living room.*

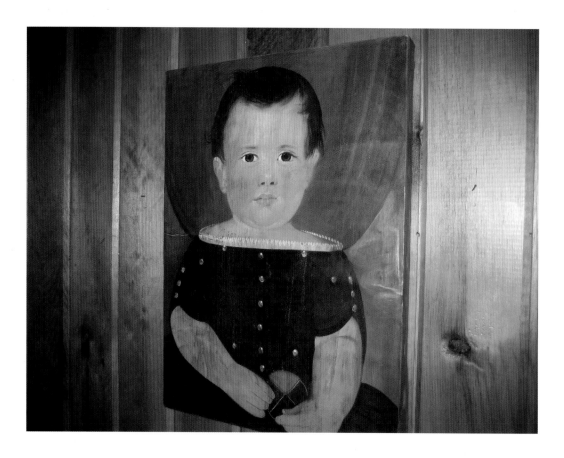

$\mathcal{M}$y travels to create this book have taken me into the homes and shops of many; all of whom willingly welcomed me into their "space" and allowed me free reign with my camera. Some of those whom I visited, I have known for years. Others, I met for the first time yet feel that our shared appreciation for the beauty of antiques and passion for country decorating have made us friends.

Everyone who contributed to this book did so by not only allowing me to photograph at will but enabled me to show and share their many talents. What I have learned is that we are generous and caring and in turn are energized by our giving to each other those ideas that feed our country heart and soul.

I am repeatedly thanked for writing the books that I do. In my mind, the real thanks goes to each of you in "our tribe" who allows us all to temporarily escape our fast-paced world and indeed travel back to a simpler time.

# Contributors

## Kyle and Nadine Brown:

Nadine Brown was hooked on antiques thirteen years ago when she purchased her first 19thC American cloth doll at a shop in Iowa City, Iowa. Since then her passion has changed from collecting mid 19thC pieces to the present where she now prefers an earlier period. Nadine has come to love 19thC New England pieces with a dry attic surface and dry original red painted pieces.

Being from Chicago originally where it was difficult to find the type of pieces she was looking for, Nadine met several dealers from the Midwest who inspired her to keep collecting at her young age despite the fact that she became tired of hearing "you're awfully young to be collecting antiques". Nadine favors rural pieces over museum quality pieces for the warmth, simplicity and loving care someone put into hand crafting them.

Two years ago, Nadine and her husband Kyle opened their own antique business called Spotted Pig Antiques. Using up much of their vacation time, they travel across country exhibiting at shows from New England to the Midwest for the passion of rural American pieces. Nadine and Kyle may be reached through their website www.spottedpigantiques.com.

## Dave and Nancy Bryer:

Nancy Bryer's maternal grandfather dismantled homes and barns for a living so as a child Nancy was introduced to early pieces and has always favored primitives. Nancy remembers her mother taking Nancy and her four siblings to flea markets, auctions and antique shops and even as a young child she loved the look and feel of early painted furniture and smalls.

David enjoys the contact with people he meets while doing antique shows. David and Nancy have done the Brimfield Show for eighteen years and a few years ago started selling at Nashville. Their son is extremely talented and accessorizes the antiques David and Nancy sell with pieces he designs and makes from old wood.

A good friend who is also an antiques dealer, told David and Nancy about an early 18thC log home in Ohio and without hesitation, David and Nancy packed their things and moved from Connecticut to the log home last year.

In addition to doing shows, Nancy and David maintain a website www.logcabincountryprimitives.com. They may be reached through their website or by email at logcabinprimitives@gmail.com

## Judy Coffey:

Judy Coffey has been a collector for over twenty-five years. When she started, Judy said she collected "poor man's antiques" – items such as a wooden advertising box thrilled her. In the past five years, Judy has found she prefers early paint and her proximity to Brimfield has enabled her to collect quite a few pieces in a relatively short period of time.

Judy has extensive collections of salt glazed stoneware, yellowware, pantry boxes and dough bowls. Many pictures of the Coffey's home will be shown in the fifth book of the "simply country" series due out in January 2009.

Judy has a shop, Country Plus, in downtown Hopkinton on Main Street. While Judy specializes in early primitives, to meet the demands and preferences of an eclectic mix of customers, Judy has devoted a section of her shop for cottage style decorating. Judy maintains a website www.countryplusonline.com and may be reached by email at countryplus@horizon.net.

The phone number at the shop is 508-435-9613

## Ronnie and Susan Derrow:

Ronnie and Susan Derrow: When Ronnie and Susan Derrow moved to their 1760 log home in 1978 from Harrisonburg Virginia, they each had full time jobs. Ronnie was a meat cutter in a local shop while Susan was a full time teacher. They moved in June and opened their shop; Shumake & Johnson within a month in one of the brick ells built in 1840. Six years later, Ronnie had to quit his job because they couldn't keep inventory stocked in the shop. Susan continued teaching until five years ago when she retired to enjoy the shop, the shows they do and her gardens. Neither one knows where Ronnie developed the skills to create the pieces he does. Perhaps it is in his genes as his grandfather was talented in the area of carpentry and Ronnie has the ability to look at something and make it. At a recent York Pennsylvania antique show, Ronnie asked Susan, "Is there anything you absolutely can't live without?" She answered, "that $2500 little stool over there". Within days, Ronnie had recreated the piece that Susan now admits to liking more than the original. Their shop is located in Mt. Sidney Virginia in the Shenandoah Valley. They are open Sat. and Sunday 12-4 or by appointment. They can be reached at 540-248-7930.

## Al and Sharon DiCampo:

Imagine being welcomed to a stranger's home with lanterns lining the walkway from the driveway to the door! That is precisely how I was greeted at the home of Al and Sharon DiCampo in Massachusetts when I arrived to photograph their home. Their hospitality didn't stop at the door. Once inside, the aroma of freshly baked cinnamon muffins filled the room and a lovely fragrant handmade soap was presented as a gift. The welcome was indicative of the entire atmosphere of their home where they have lived for over twenty years.

Each room was a joy to enter and capture on film. It became apparent that Sharon likes to decorate small spaces and in each nook and cranny I found another small antique box or basket filled with decorations or vignettes. Oftentimes homes decorated in an early period are uncomfortable to live in, but that was not the case in Al and Sharon's home. Soft chairs, a warm fire and an early decorated but workable kitchen made the home very cozy.

Sharon and Al have collected antiques for a number of years and have continued to enjoy earlier pieces as time goes by. Many pictures of the DiCampo's home will be featured in the 4th book, *Country Decorating for All Seasons*.

Sharon is an avid gardener and her grounds are patterned after those at Sturbridge Village. Covered with snow, only the contours were visible but even in the dead of winter, it was easy to imagine how magnificent they must be.

Although Sharon does not have a business, she does offer pieces on consignment at The Barn Bowl Shop in Douglas which is owned by her friend Louise Villa.

## Bruce and Stacee Droit:

The Droits are most likely known as the owners of Arnette's Country Store. The family business was started by Stacee's parents in 1976 and has continued to be recognized worldwide. Stacee grew up helping her mother sew while Stacee's brother Darren helped their father carve the faces of the dolls.

Arnette's Country Store is best known for their dolls, antique reproductions and one of a kind handmade country accessories. Their dolls have become collector items with the most popular being the black dolls. Stacee and her employees also create other primitive accessories such as their soft Santas and pull toys and their Christmas line has become the most popular in the last few years. Stacee has continued to create the same high-quality pieces that her mother did when she started the business. As Stacee says "we strive to maintain that country feeling in all that we do. After all, it is my heritage".

Bruce and Stacee sell their handmade pieces through regional and national trade shows and are usually sold out within the first hour. Located in Illinois, they also have a retail business as well as a website www.arnettescountrystore.com. Stacee may be reached through her website or www.picturetrail.com/arnettescountrystore

## Dave and Twila Fairbanks:

Dave and Twila Fairbanks of Roca Nebraska attribute their love of log homes to years of having lived in Kentucky and Colorado. When September 11th occurred, they both knew they wanted to move back to the prairies of Nebraska and closer to their family. In 2002 they built "the little log cabin" in which they lived while Dave and crew built the large square log home.

Twila has been in the antique business for over thirty years and clearly remembers the first antique she purchased: a trunk with her maiden name on the front which research proved belonged to a great aunt. Twila continues to prefer the more primitive American country style antique that shows authentic signs of craftsmanship and use.

The "little log home" became a shop, Log Cabin Primitives and Prairie Woolworks in 2003. In the shop, Twila sells antiques and offers classes in rug hooking and wool appliqué.

Last fall, Dave and Twila moved the shop into the walk-out basement of the large log home and converted the "little log home" into a bed and breakfast called The Log Cabin Inn.

Twila can be reached through her website at www.prairiewoolworks.com.

## Bob Jessen and Jim Hohnwald:

Bob Jessen and Jim Hohnwald have been in the antique business for over twenty-eight years specializing in 18th and 19thC American, country furniture in original paint. Both being from the Midwest where early homes weren't early enough for them, they had been searching for an 18thC home in New England for years. While vacationing in Florida, they received a call from their agent saying she had the house that fit their requirements. Bob and Jim flew to Boston immediately and drove through a Nor'easter on back roads to New Hampshire. Jim's initial reaction was one of disappointment but Bob convinced Jim that since they had come all this way, they should at least take a look inside. As Jim says, by the time they got to the kitchen and saw the sheathing, he was sold and they subsequently owned the house within days. The home they purchased happens to be the oldest home in Fitzwilliam. Bob and Jim do the premier New Hampshire Dealer Show, Nashville and numerous shows throughout Ohio. They sell from their home as well. In addition to early American country furniture, they also specialize in unusual treenware, early lighting, textiles, painted baskets and folk art. They are open year round by appointment only. Call 603-585-9188 for directions, as there is no business sign. They may also be reached through their website www.bobjessenjimhohnwald.com

## Al and Ann Kuehn:

Al and Ann Kuehn of Greenwood South Carolina are the second family out of the original family to live in their 1800's farmhouse. The property known as High Grove Farm was originally a cotton farm. The farmhouse has eleven fireplaces including one in an upstairs bathroom. On the property are a number of outbuildings including a cabin that once was the cook's quarters. This cabin is now Ann's shop. Another outbuilding is the sheep barn – home to Lucy, Daisy and Buttercup.

When Ann and Al moved to the farm, Ann fell in love with the cook's cabin and thus Straw Broom Primitives was born. The name Straw Broom is in memory of Ann's grandmother who used a straw broom to sweep her porches.

Twelve years ago, with three friends, Ann hosted her first antique show on the grounds of the farmhouse and cabin. Now over seventy dealers with more than 1500 people traveling for hundreds of miles attend the one-day show.

Straw Broom is open Thursday – Saturday 10-4. Since the shop is on the property, Ann is willing to welcome customers by calling ahead. Ann can be reached through her website www.picturetrail.com/strawbroomprimitives

## Rich and Melanie Lortie:

Rich and Melanie Lortie of Massachusetts have the unique good fortune to both enjoy creating furnishings for their home and it is evident in every room you enter. Rich enjoys building furniture as a hobby and when he has completed the "construction," Melanie does the finishing work. Although Rich prefers the William and Mary period and Melanie prefers more country pieces, they've found the means to compromise and the end result is a warm eclectic home.

Rich and Melanie built their saltbox colonial home seven years ago and since then have become avid collectors due to the number of shops in their vicinity. When not gardening, Melanie paints floor cloths, stencils rooms, makes curtains and pillows. Rich's escape during nice weather is the golf course.

Although Melanie doesn't have a shop of her own, she places items for sale on consignment in The Barn Bowl in Douglas owned by Louise Villa.

## Shannon McConnachie:

What started as a hobby for Shannon McConnachie from Arkansas and a means to decorate her home has developed into a successful business Sweet Liberty Homestead. Shannon's creative talents have earned her recognition in Early American Life magazine and as a power seller on ebay. Shannon is in the process of writing a book on primitive folk art dolls that will provide patterns as well as pictures. She will sell her book through country shops and through ebay. Shannon may be reached through her ebay store at Sweetlibertyhomestead or by phone at 501-941-0093.

## Ralph and Linda Miller:

Ralph and Linda Miller have lived with antiques since they were married almost forty years ago. When first married, they were given family cast offs to help them establish a home and in the late 1970's became serious about furnishing their home in authentic pieces when they attended their first auction. Their first antique, a hand painted bowl by an itinerant artist started them on the path to what would eventually become a full-time business for Linda as the proprietor of The Miller House Antiques.

Initially Ralph and Linda rented space at a shop in Powell Ohio while selling their pieces at shows as well. Over the years, their taste in antiques has evolved from an eclectic mix to a passion for primitives. Ten years ago they realized their dream when they purchased their 1806 log home that had been used as a trading post with the Indians and which had been moved

from between the Licking and Muskingum Rivers to the present site in 1995 by the previous owners.

Ralph still works as a Consulting Engineer but Linda has retired as a school secretary so that she can devote time to her business. They are in the process of creating a website but until it is ready, Linda may be reached at 614-833-2521 or by email at millerhouse8739@sbcglobal.net. The Miller House Antiques is open by appointment only so calling ahead is a necessity.

## Sandy and Jim O'Connor:

Sandy O'Connor never knew what country decorating was all about until she walked into the former American Heritage Shop in South Kent Connecticut. That was ten years ago. Since that time, Sandy has become a die-hard country antique collector and their lake home on Bantam Lake in Connecticut reflects her new style. The Lake House, as they call it, was built last year on property leased from White Memorial, an environmental conservatory in Litchfield County. Both Jim and Sandy are retired and built the Lake House as a family home for their children and grandchildren to enjoy on the water. Although Jim and Sandy don't have a shop or sell antiques, they continue to travel to add and upgrade their collections.

## Roger and Pam Parker:

Since moving to Billerica Massachusetts ten years ago, Pam and her husband Roger have found wonderful shops and markets in the area in which to shop. As a result, they've developed an interest in antiques and have remodeled their home even to the extent of changing walls and moving stairways. When you approach their home, you walk through well-manicured gardens on a brick path to the door. Off to the other side of the driveway is a small outbuilding decorated for the holidays that I will be showing in the next book, Country Decorating for All Seasons.

Roger, a self-employed electrician, is handy at everything according to Pam. They have been actively involved in the remodeling process from the start.

When not working in their home or out antiquing together, Pam helps Roger with the business and loves to garden.

## Paul and Jean Peterson:

Jean Peterson is the first woman I have known who has collected antiques since she was a teenager. Descended from a sea captain, Jean spent time at her maternal grandparents home in Hyannis on Cape Cod. She was fascinated by the stories she was told and the history of her family. Although her taste has evolved from having collected china and Victorian style pieces to a preference for primitive and country formal today, Jean has not lost her passion for the history. As a preservationist, Jean's love of history is such that when she holds an early piece, she feels a spiritual bond with the previous owners and strives to convey that interest to newcomers.

Jean, originally from Cranston, Rhode Island, was widowed at an early age and has since remarried to Paul, now retired from General Dynamics. Twenty years ago, while taking a drive through Douglas, Massachusetts, they stumbled onto their present home. It appeared to be vacant and, after turning into the driveway they discovered a "for sale" sign buried in the snow. Once Jean determined that there was a large, intact fireplace behind the panels covering the fireplace, she was sold.

The first year was a year of total restoration of their 1740 Georgian home with a full-time professional restorer on site. They indeed uncovered not only a large fireplace, but an area on the second floor where runaway slaves were once concealed. Since then, Jean and Paul have done extensive research and learned that the house was originally owned by Dr. William Jennison who served both Mendon and Douglas followed by the Rev. Isaac Stone, second pastor of the First Congregational Church. Paul and Jean are the sixth owners and have appropriately named the house, The Jennison-Stone House. Further research indicates that their home was one of the houses where meetings were held during the early years of the formation of the Town. The second owner, Isaac Stone was instrumental in establishing the Town's first library.

Jean operates an antique shop at her home on Main Street and is open on Fridays and Saturdays or by appointment. She may be reached at 508-476-7011 or by email Peterson. p@verizon.net. Tours of her home located in the historic district of Douglas are available.

## Paul and Connie Pudelka:

Connie loves everything having to do with history, hearth or home and it shows in the home she has created and the pieces she loves to collect. Her husband Paul, with the help of their two sons Heath and Tommy, built their log home in the woods of Connecticut twenty-two years ago. Paul, a contractor, has the inherent talent to be able to see something or take Connie's design and build it. Connie works with Paul as he builds each piece and then does the finishing. Connie simply has to ask and the piece is sitting in the house ready to decorate and enjoy that evening.

It isn't often that we are fortunate enough to surround ourselves at home and work with the things we enjoy most, but Connie is one of those people who has been able to do just that. Connie's first job was working at The Seraph with Alex Pifer whom Connie credits with having introduced her to 18thC pieces and exposing her to exceptional reproductions. When The Seraph closed, Connie went to work at The American Heritage Shop owned by her long time friend Kathy Trabucco. That experience was a blessing in that it has allowed her to be part of a business she loves while able to fill her home with great treasures. The real bonus Connie feels is the long lasting friendships she has made over the years with people who share her love of history, hearth and home.

Connie may be reached at logcabinprimitives@sbcglobal.net. or 203-748-7761. Connie currently sells on ebay under the id ctlogcabin

## Bill Quinn:

Bill Quinn has been in the antique business for over twenty years and concentrates on buying and selling pieces which have exceptional color and surface. Bill gravitates towards those antiques that show natural wear through years of honest use. If it doesn't look used, Bill won't buy it and avoids any piece that has been repainted or touched up. What that means is that Bill's inventory is primitive and it's that charm and warmth of those pieces which Bill appreciates.

Bill takes regular buying trips and often sells out of his inventory before he's had a chance to move it into his shop. Bill moved his shop a few years ago from Wiscasset Maine to his home in Alna just ten minutes away. Although Bill sells primarily to dealers and decorators, he's available for retail business by calling 207-586-5134. Bill's shop, Bill Quinn Antiques, is located in the natural setting of his wooded property and gardens and is a must see if you are in the area.

## Anita and Gerry Ramsey:

When Gerry was transferred from Ohio thirteen years ago, he and his wife Anita headed east and relocated in Pennsylvania. Shortly after their transfer, the company where Gerry worked closed and Anita and Gerry found themselves unemployed. In 1996, they purchased a small retail business dealing with initially small reproduction home accessories. As the business grew, more space was needed and in 2001, they found an historic farmhouse built in 1835 by Charles Shimer, son of John Shimer, the founder of Shimerville, Pennsylvania. Charles Shimer was the proprietor of the old Shimerville Hotel located on what was the first public road in Lehigh Valley. The historic property was ideal for their shop.

The property consists of the farmhouse, a circa 1770 stone bank barn and a summer kitchen which had been used to prepare food for the hotel. Their shop, Aunt Daisy's , is filled with handcrafted country furniture accessories, most of which are made by local artisans. Aunt Daisy's is located in Emmaus Pennsylvania. Gerry and Anita may be reached at 610-967-0552 or by email through their website www.auntdaisys.com

## Ruth Rochelle:

Ruth realized a long time dream when she started her business The Primitive Homeplace on their property in Bradford Tennessee. I included many pictures of Ruth and Jimmy's primitive home in my previous book Of Hearth and Home – Simply Country and with the recent creation of their buttery and tavern room, I asked if I could share some pictures of their new space.

Ruth and Jimmy travel extensively to ensure that her shop is filled with country primitives and accessories. The

Primitive Homeplace is open Wednesday – Saturday 10-4 or by appointment. Ruth may be reached through the Internet at ruthprimitives@hotmail.com.or through her website www.picturetrail.com/primitivehomeplace

## Bea Sparrow:

Bea Sparrow, owner of Old Glory in Waynesville, Ohio, has been in the antique business for ten years. Her shop now has 3600 square feet including the new "wing" that was recently added. The shop is in a constant state of flux and Bea's clientele come from throughout the United States and even as far away as Nova Scotia. Although, there are some 18thC pieces, approximately fifty percent of Bea's merchandise is 19thC and fifty percent are replica pieces. Bea works with Donny and Sally Wimms who have mastered the technique of creating custom designed kitchens resembling those of the 19thC period. The surface has been painted in such a way that the best of experts have difficulty discerning what is an authentic 19thC piece and what is a Whims built piece. Old Glory is open six days 10-5 and closed on Monday. Bea may be reached via email through her website www.oldegloryshops.com

## Carolyn Thompson:

Carolyn Thompson has been in love with antiques since a young child and is always looking for ways to transform her home into an early 18thC New England look. The pictures of her home found in my second book Of Hearth and Home – Simply Country were so popular that I was asked to include her again in future books.

Carolyn offers exceptional primitive accessories that are handcrafted by her friend Dawn and sells at a number of shows including Heart O Country in Nashville.

Carolyn maintains a website www.carolynthompsonprimitives.com and may be emailed through that site.

## Louise Villa:

Louise Villa and I met through a mutual friend and it was an instantaneous friendship! During a driving snowstorm, I ventured to her home just south of Worcester, Massachusetts and received the warmest welcome from Louise and her husband, Bud. While Bud and Louise's home is a newly constructed saltbox colonial, once inside the door ,you step back to the early 19thC.

Many pictures of the Villa home were shown in my second book Of Hearth and Home – Simply Country and I couldn't resist sharing pictures of their master bedroom in A Simpler Time. I was fortunate to visit Louise and Bud during the holidays and will include many more pictures of their home decorated for the holidays in the fourth book Country Decorating for All Seasons.

Louise operates a business at her home, The Bowl Barn, in Douglas Massachusetts. She may be reached at 508-476-1355

## Additional Resources:

- Milltown Primitives: Shop owner Robin Rock 27 Coogan Blvd #17C Mystic, Connecticut 860-572-1830

- Murals: Susan Dwyer, East Greenwich RI 401-398-0646 www.susandwyerartworks.com

- Primitive Homeplace: Shop owner Ruth Rochelle, 240 Olivers Chapel Road, Bradford, TN

- Itinerant Painter: Gladys Desmond 401-568-9263

- Family Heirloom Weavers: Red Lion PA 717-246-5797

- Good Old Days Country Shop: Pultneyville NY 315-589-2775 www.goodolddayscountryshop.com

- The Keeping Room: 9 West Street Douglas MA 508-476-7798

- Barn Bowl Antiques: Louise Villa, Shop Owner 508-476-1355

- Primitives: hand forged iron by Kathy Nugent 913-897-9411 nugentgbc@yahoo.com